MARK OESTREICHER
& BROOKLYN LINDSEY

A
PARENT'S
GUIDE

TO UNDERSTANDING

TEENAGE GIRLS

*REMEMBERING WHO SHE WAS,
CELEBRATING WHO SHE'S BECOMING*

simply for parents

A Parent's Guide to Understanding Teenage Girls

Remembering Who She Was, Celebrating Who She's Becoming

© 2012 Mark Oestreicher and Brooklyn Lindsey

group.com
simplyyouthministry.com

Credits

Authors: Mark Oestreicher and Brooklyn Lindsey
Executive Developer: Nadim Najm
Chief Creative Officer: Joani Schultz
Copy Editor: Rob Cunningham
Cover Art and Production: Veronica Preston

ISBN 978-0-7644-8460-5

10 9 8 7 6 5 4 3 2 1   20 19 18 17 16 15 14 13 12

Printed in the United States of America.

CONTENTS

TEENAGE GIRLS

CHAPTER 1:
SHE'S CHANGING

Time for a checkup (don't worry, it's free and won't be billed to your insurance). Do you ever feel like this: What happened to my little girl?

I (Brooklyn) have two daughters, aged 2 and 5. I read parenting advice and try to keep up with where they should be developmentally. From the day they were born, I've kept a record of every pound they gained, the arrival of each and every tooth, and each sitting, crawling, walking, jumping, climbing milestone that came along. I've also watched them transition from liquids to solids, cribs to beds, diapers to big-girl pants. I even try to write down the funny things they say so I'll remember someday and be able to tell them all about it. Even when I'm prepared for all of these things, the changes still continue to catch me off guard like 3 o'clock summer afternoon rains in central Florida. I know they're coming, but they still sneak up on me and catch me unprepared.

My 2-year-old daughter, Mya, recently decided to transition from a blankie and a baby in bed at night, to wanting a harmonica and an extra pair of underwear. Random. Before she goes to bed she plays a little tune. And I guess it's sort of comforting that she has a backup plan in place (with the extra training pants) just in case she needs help.

It seems perfectly normal that our toddlers would do outlandish things. We don't understand why they suddenly feel more comforted by a harmonica (really, a harmonica?) than by the blanket they've slept with their entire life—but because they are babies, we give them space to grow and change.

It's the same with our teenage daughters. They still need the same kind of noticeable attention. While the milestones and checkups change, it's still important to make much of them and help girls through the things they can't get their minds around.

I (Marko) have an 18-year-old daughter, a senior in high school. I'm at the tail end of this ride. Liesl is an amazing young woman: articulate and creative, passionate and compassionate. But she still surprises me, in both good and frustrating ways. In fact, these days, as she's very much taking the "I'm independent" bull by the horns, I'm blindsided by surprises multiple times each week. Most of these surprises are encouraging. Others are maddening. Some are both!

Other than the first few years of life, teenage girls are going through the most dramatic developmental changes they'll ever experience. And they need us to be there, just as present and involved as we were when they could sleep on our chests and climb into our beds.

There have been many moments in youth ministry when each of us has come into the youth building and noticed girls that we no longer recognize. They are girls we've known since they were little. We've hung out at all hours, painted each other's nails (well, Brooklyn has), laughed, cried, wrestled with ideas—and then they changed.

It seems to happen overnight, in a flash, like those rags-to-riches princess changeovers you might see on Broadway—except that when the smoke clears, you have no idea what you'll find. It feels just that quick, the experience when we notice that she isn't the same, that she looks, acts, and responds differently than she did before. (And by "she," we mean *all* of them.)

When did this change happen? Sometime between seventh and eighth grades (sooner for some, later for some) her body, mind, and emotions start to change. Suddenly, she becomes a wonderfully unique person who can hold a conversation, can get passionate about things she cares about, and can make some decisions on her own.

As youth workers, we're often grieved when this change starts. It's not the tragedy kind of grief, but more the "We feel like our puppy just ran away" sort of grief, because we see her growing and separating herself from the identity that used to depend almost exclusively on her parents and, to a lesser extent, on us.

Of course, the feelings we experience with countless teenage girls in our ministries are nothing compared to the feelings of seeing this change occur in your own daughter.

It's the strangest combination of loss and gain: It feels like you've just lost the best thing that ever happened to you, yet you've also gained the best thing that ever happened to you. And it can cause us to react in crazy ways, if we aren't ready for it.

So, where do we start in our understanding?

Start with what you know.

Think about where your daughter is in her life.

It might be helpful to map it out. Draw a timeline from the year she was born to the current year. Mark significant milestones above the line. And think about her life from the point of view of someone who is only now just getting to know her.

Outside of her adolescent development, do you see any themes in her life? Have there been things out of her control that have shaped the person you see her becoming?

Before you begin to understand, share dreams, and launch her to live them, you need to know her—really know her.

Sometimes teenagers will tell you outright that they don't want you, as a parent, to know them. But our experience tells us that it's mostly a smokescreen, a front put up as part of her necessary and good journey toward becoming who God made her to be.

Think back to the timeline again:

When did God become more than a name for her? *Has* God become more than a name for her?

Where does she sit at the dinner table? How does she communicate with you?

How does she decide what to wear?

What things seem to set her off, frustrate her, or cause conflict between you? Is there an underlying source of pain fueling these things?

You really don't need to try to psychoanalyze her, but asking these questions will help you to get a broader perspective and to begin thinking about what she carries with her as she develops into her own person.

Now, think about the outward changes she's going through.

When did they start?

What did you notice first?

Puberty can start as early as 9 years old! It's important to recognize when these changes begin. Oftentimes, the emotions accompanying menarche (a girl's first menstrual period) start before it happens. Knowing this helps you to see the cycle and embrace it as a healthy part of her development without being completely frustrated with her changing moods.

Another way to start thinking about your daughter is to consider where she is in processing the three primary "tasks" of adolescence—tasks she'll be working on throughout her middle school and high school years (and often into her young adult years).

- Identity ("Who am I?"): How has she been answering this question in front of you? in front of her friends?

- Autonomy ("How am I unique, and how do my choices matter?"): Do you see her trying out different things? How does she handle responsibility? Do you see her taking ownership in new areas of her life?

- Affinity ("Where and to whom do I belong?"): Are there places where she gravitates more than others? Is she forming a strong sense of belonging? How is that place (or those places) of belonging informing her identity?

There are many more questions you could ask yourself; these are just the tip of the iceberg when it comes to your daughter. Remember, it's not about knowing the *answers*. It's about understanding *her*. And that happens with an intentional movement to see her, notice her changes, listen, look, think about her, and pray for her.

We hope you'll use this book as an opportunity to understand your posture in front of your daughter and to let it help you deconstruct some of your assumptions and misunderstandings. Then, from a place of wholeness and trust (in a God who loves you and is passionate about your parenting), you can start to see your daughter for who she is and who she's becoming.

Who Is This Girl?

"One day that little girl that cried whenever you left her and would light up whenever you walked into the room, will not want you around or hear a thing you have to say. Go through these years with patient understanding of your new role in her life, and one day you will open that door and your girl will be back, and she will have learned so much since the time when she knew it all."
—Christy; Southlake, Texas

Raising teenagers is no walk in the park. It takes guts, patience, a willingness to stay present in the everyday chaos that's naturally a part of adolescence, and—maybe most importantly—a daily, active faith that God is working a miracle.

Every now and then, a superbly balanced teenage girl comes through our ministries. It's like the light of heaven shines directly on her. She seems to always demonstrate kindness, she's the first to offer to help, she's doing great in school, and she even likes hanging out with her parents!

When we observe these rare girls, we almost always assume it's because of amazing parenting. We seek out her parents and ask, "You are such great parents; can you share the secret parenting sauce with all of us?" Most often, these parents look at us with bewilderment and say, "We don't know! It surely can't be because of us!" Then, almost inevitably, sometime in the future, the veil is dropped and those same parents come back with tears in their eyes, frustration in their voices, and every form of communication their daughter owns locked in their car.

What happened? Why is she responding so differently? Where did the heavenly girl go? It's like aliens abducted their real daughter and harnessed forces of evil to control her moods and decisions.

Ever felt that way?

Not every teenage girl goes through emotional aerobics, not every girl gets nasty and mean, not every girl has problems with friends, not every girl has a change in her attitudes toward authority. But every girl does change. Knowing this as a parent, expecting it, and doing your best to see the changes through some great question-asking lenses will help you as you experience these changes alongside her.

We like how Ginny Olson puts it in her book *Teenage Girls* (Zondervan/Youth Specialties, 2006):

During this phase of her life, change is the only constant; every relationship is shifting, and every belief is questioned. What she once knew as solid ground now feels as though an earthquake hit it. She's not quite sure where to find the stability of her childhood, or if she even wants to. In the midst of this chaos, she's screaming the question of adolescence, "Who am I?" and a whole series of other questions…Who is she in relationship to her friends? To her family? To her community? She's seeking to find her identity.

Like the parents who end up in our offices (honestly, *most* parents would end up in our offices if they had time), you may feel moments of helplessness. You may feel like curling up in a ball and crying like a baby because what she said to you on the phone was one of the most hurtful things you've ever heard. You may look at her and say, "Who is this girl?" And this is when you realize that your own faith is the only thing that's going to carry you through.

A mom that I (Brooklyn) know well, after raising two daughters (and two sons!), offers this advice:

"Above all else, make certain that your own spiritual life is where it should be. Be ever in the Word and on your knees praying for wisdom. God doesn't promise raising your daughter will be a bed of roses, but when you get stuck in the thorns, he will take your pain and turn it into something beautiful."—Natalie; Logan, Ohio

Intentional Engagement

So what do you do in the meantime (in between banging your head against the wall and praying)?

Enjoy her.

Sit with that one for a moment. Can you distance yourself from the fear and confusion long enough to enjoy her?

Look for ways you can learn new things about your daughter. She doesn't even know everything about herself yet, so you won't be able to learn everything. But strive to discover things about her that will help her answer the questions she's asking, such as:

Who am I?

What's my relationship with my parents supposed to look like?

What's my role in my community? Do I matter?

Who are my friends, really? What role do they play in my life?

She'll be changing quickly and going through plenty of extremes. However, if you're taking the time and putting effort into getting to know her over and over again, it will pay off.

You might be thinking, "But she won't let me get within a hundred yards of her world. How am I supposed to get to know her when she doesn't even want me around?"

That's a great question, so whether you asked it or not, let's talk about some ways you can be a part of the changes she is going through without becoming the helicopter parent of the year—who hovers and intrudes but doesn't engage.

Get involved before the changes occur. It's always easier to stay involved in her life than to suddenly start involvement when your daughter is 16.

Watch for early physical signs of change. When you notice evidence that puberty has begun, don't ignore the signs; celebrate puberty's arrival in a way that would honor her and make her feel special. (Dads: Of course, your experience of these physical changes will be different from a mom's, but you can still pay attention to the early signs of your daughter's entry into adolescence.) For moms, this might means taking your daughter to get a manicure and talking to her about the approaching changes. For dads, this might mean buying her flowers and setting up a time to tell her how much you love her and how happy you are with the young woman she's about to become.

When my daughter (Marko here) had her first period, we actually had a "period party" for her! We took her out of school for a day, got her a massage and a new haircut, and took her out to dinner. We were intentional about celebrating her budding womanhood without making it weird or awkward, but also without ignoring this significant milestone.

Look for opportunities to have conversations about friendship. This is thin ice, of course, as you can easily come across as intrusive, or like you're interrogating her. The trick is to focus more on asking questions (and being genuinely interested in the answers), rather than attempting to get your opinions heard. If you ask good, open questions, you'll often find that your daughter will, at some point, express a conundrum or some tension she's processing. That's your opportunity to affirm the tension and to ask if she'd like to hear how you have dealt with the same tension in your own friendships. More often than not, if you've created a safe environment for this conversation, she'll be interested in hearing your experience (more than your platitudes or directives).

Notice and encourage competencies. The default parenting approach for so many people, often anchored in fear, is to parent by control. But the best parenting is less interested in control and more interested in facilitation: helping a girl identify and nurture her unique gifts and passions and means of contributing to something greater than herself.

Serve together. Whenever you can, show how putting others first gives you life and meaning, even when life feels dull and meaningless. The two of us have seen over and over again how parents and teenagers who find ways to serve alongside each other have the strongest relationships. You can model a way of living for your daughter in a way that you could never accomplish with words alone.

Help her feel safe. There's a tension with this one. On one hand, it couldn't be more critical that your daughter feels safe in your home and in her relationship with you. A teenager experiences plenty of unsafe feelings in her rapidly expanding world, and your home and relationship can become a beautiful haven where she can truly be herself without constantly worrying about whether people will like her or not. But one of the problems the two of us often see in parenting today is how *overly* protective parents are of their teenage children. Your daughter needs experiences that *aren't* controlled in order to grow. Safety, yes; control, no. (We're not suggesting that's simple, by the way.)

This might be a tough statement for you to believe, but we're asking you to trust us. We have 40 years (combined) of experience working with thousands of teenage girls, and research backs this up: Teenagers *want* and *need* boundaries. They thrive with appropriate independence *within* clearly defined boundaries.

Here's another one that might be tough for you to swallow (but we can affirm with experience and research): Teenagers *want* their parents involved in their lives. Your daughter might give you every signal possible that this isn't true, but that isn't the full story. Those "pushing away from you" signals are merely her important and good efforts at learning about the extent of her power. Don't throw in the towel by misreading her deepest desires.

There isn't a one-to-one correlation between happy and healthy teenage girls and parents who clearly set boundaries and stay engaged. But it has to be, from what we've seen, a close correlation. Sure, we've seen plenty of fantastic parents who work to set boundaries and deeply desire to stay engaged but whose daughters still go off the deep end in one way or another. And we've seen disengaged parents who set zero boundaries but the teenage girl is a paragon of awesomeness. But those examples are both exceptions, and not the norm.

If your daughter is already a teenager, you only have another lap or two around the parenting track. Your role (while still a parent, of course) will shift dramatically as your daughter reaches the end of her teen years. So re-up your commitment to walk (or run!) these laps with intentionality, generosity, love, and presence.

"Every day at dinner, my parents eat quietly while I walk them through my 10-hour day. They think nothing of it, but whenever something big happens (irritating teachers, impossible tests, idiotic friends), I spend the rest of my day preparing the story to tell them that night."
—Sarah; Lexington, Massachusetts

Some Body

"In my experience, it is the good girls, the dutiful daughters and high achievers who are at the greatest risk for anorexia."
—Dr. Mary Pipher,
Reviving Ophelia *(Riverhead Trade, 2005)*

We could hardly overstate the importance of how your daughter sees her own body and how she thinks other people see her body. Being aware of body image issues will help you see more quickly when your daughter struggles with them.

Not only is your daughter's body changing, but the amount of time and effort she spends noticing other people's bodies is changing, too. She'll compare herself with girls her age. And she'll compare herself with "perfect" strangers she sees on TV and in magazines.

She's also noticing guys more. (Some of you are thinking, "Thanks for the brilliant insight, captains of the obvious!") The posters in her room shift from horses and kittens to teenage heartthrobs from her favorite movie or TV series.

This might crack you up: The word *estrogen* (the hormone rampaging through your daughter's body right now) is formed from two words, *estrus* and *gen*. Its root meaning is "to generate estrus." Estrus (ready for this?) means "frenzied passion"! This may be the last thing in the world we want for our daughters as their bodies and minds go through such swift changes!

Estrogens are actually a group of hormones produced by the ovaries, and they're strategic to a girl's development of secondary sex characteristics, such as breast and pubic hair growth. They also heighten her sense of smell, which is most sensitive halfway between her periods.

As you may have discovered already, once puberty begins, the differences in your daughter can become drastic. And now her body is setting her up to experience "frenzied passion" and causing her to have a freakishly perceptive sense of smell.

It can be overwhelming to think about all she's going through physically. But the biggest, most important parenting practice, when considering the *physical* changes going on inside your daughter's body, is to look for ways to love her unconditionally. Get beyond acne breakouts, rapid growth, and gangly awkwardness to see who she's becoming on the inside.

If your daughter is maturing early, don't be fooled into thinking she doesn't need your help (in fact, girls who mature early often need *extra* help from Mom and Dad). She might *look* mature, but that doesn't mean she is. Girls who physically mature early often receive confusing and unwanted attention. And in possibly the most unfair of all teenage judgments, they are often considered sexually loose by their peers (both girls and guys).

If your daughter is maturing later, reassure her that everyone matures at a different pace, and comfort her when she gets impatient. Remind her that she'll soon be on the road and will quickly catch up to her peers. Above all, remind her that God looks at the heart—it's the most important growth that will happen for her. The seeds of courage and character being planted in her heart will far outshine the outward signs of her maturation.

Going into the sixth grade, there were only a few things I (Brooklyn) was worried about. First, having a white pair of leather K-Swiss™ shoes. They were the shoes that most girls showed up wearing on the first day of school (or so I'd heard). Second, not getting a scary teacher. And third, being able to find my locker and remember the combination. That was all.

The first month of sixth grade wasn't too bad. I don't remember much, just that I was there. But it didn't take long for me to start noticing the girls who were already wearing bras. It also didn't take long for me to figure out that I was a GIANT towering over really cute but little guys. I must have seemed like a monster from their perspective. My growth spiked in the sixth grade, continuing all the way into the eighth grade. I grew nearly 7 inches over the course of about two years. It was like a death sentence—no chance of getting a date to the dance.

I (Marko) remember when my daughter, about 15, decided she wanted a super-edgy haircut: a subtle Mohawk. Deciding it wasn't a fight on which we wanted to spend our parenting chips, my wife and I let her make this decision. She was very proud of it, for a couple of months. But I remember intensely the day she cried and told us that she "didn't feel pretty anymore" and wanted to grow her hair back.

Knowing how awkward and significant these body image changes are gives us a lot of empathy for teenage girls. And, once again, we can see how *critically important* their parents' voices and affirmation are during these shifts. Bottom line for moms: Your verbal processing with your daughter about these issues is irreplaceable. Bottom line for dads: Your regularly communicated affection and unconditional acceptance is irreplaceable.

I Think I Can

My (Brooklyn) youth ministry has an honesty box. A few times a year we give teenagers cards and ask them to write down any question they want to ask. They can ask *anything*. It's anonymous, and we encourage them to write something that they really are wondering about and may be a little embarrassed or ashamed to ask. Because there's a box for the girls and a box for the guys, we are able to organize our answers around the hot points.

For our middle school girls, the biggest and most pressing questions center around clothing. Is it is a sin to wear short shorts? How short is too short?

For our middle school guys, well, they basically want to know how *things* work. And by *things*, I mean sex.

We see their curiosity and creativity coming out in exercises like this, as well as their budding desire to challenge conventions as part of figuring things out. Many of the girls don't write down their opinions, but I know it to be true because of conversations we've had. If a girl were being really honest, she might have written, "My parents think my shorts are too short. I don't. I need some biblical evidence that they're not too short, so I can keep wearing them."

Ask high school girls for gut-level honest questions, and the flavor has changed. Some still ask "help me disagree with my parents" questions, but many are wondering how to get out of messes they've made since junior high. Or they want to know how to help a friend who is in a mess of her own. They really are thinking and trying to discern. But we know their base for decision-making is inexperienced, in process, and incomplete. That's why parents play such an important role. Teenagers are lacking in development of the brain's frontal lobe, the decision-making center of the brain. Parents need to be "surrogate frontal lobes." Otherwise— in the midst of this pivotal time of learning to understand moods, plan ahead, weigh choices, and control impulses— they'll be on their own, influenced by peers and media in deciding which way to turn.

CHAPTER 2: SHE'S FOLLOWING

Her Greatest Influence: You!

"When our daughter got to eighth grade, a switch flipped overnight. Our compliant, people-pleasing daughter disappeared and another version of her was born that we didn't know as well. We had to relearn how to communicate with her. We had always walked in front of her and removed all the dangers and insisted she comply, which she did. But now we had to learn to walk beside her and still hold her hand through the tough times, but also be willing to allow her to trip and fall and experience some of life's difficulties firsthand. We had to take the shield away a little bit."
—Brett (married to Mindy); Lakeland, Florida

"Just a theory: As moms we tend to use many more words over the years to communicate with our daughters than their fathers use. At some point, our voices may tend to sound like 'blah, blah, blah' to these precious girls. However, a father's words tend to have more weight at times, because when the man in their life speaks, the

daughters are hungrier to stop and listen to what they have to say."
—Mindy (married to Brett); Lakeland, Florida

Brooklyn here. Growing up, my mother always told me she believed in me and that I could do anything I set my mind to. Looking back, I'm sure she said this knowing fully that she couldn't pay for my college, she couldn't unbreak my heart, she couldn't ensure that I got my dream job or career, and she certainly couldn't rewire my brain to think mathematically. Even when all odds felt against me (like the time a boy broke my heart one summer, and I was sobbing in my room) and even though my mom was going through her own heartbreak, she still managed to invest in me with her encouragement: "You can do this, you can get through this." Somehow she made me feel like I was actually capable, that I was really getting through it (and I was). She was right there with me all along. And when things got really difficult to manage, when she felt my needs were beyond her, she took me to church, believing that I could find additional voices of support there. When she couldn't give us the friend support we needed, she found a place where support would be provided.

My mom, even though I didn't realize it at the time, was (and continues to be) a great influence in my life. She built up a belief in me that God is able and that I can do anything—if I believe.

It's a sweet story. But it's more than a story—it's an illustration of a reality that's been proved by research: You are the most important influence in your daughter's life. This is particularly true in the area of faith. Researchers have gone so far as to say that the single best indicator of a teenager's faith is the faith of her parents.

If your daughter sees, in everyday ways, that you value your faith, it's likely she will do likewise. If you *live out* your faith, she will likely do the same. This correlation has less to do with what you *say* about the importance of your faith, and more to do with what she sees you *live out* in your life. So, if you model an example of honesty in your home and outside, you provide a living laboratory for her to test her own values.

This also means that you wade through moments of dishonesty with courage and hope. Recently, I (Marko) lied to my daughter about something minor. I instantly felt horrible about it, on so many levels. Frankly, I felt stupid and incompetent, realizing both that I wasn't modeling what I wanted for my daughter and that it was going to be awkward confessing to her. But I knew I was at a critical teaching moment, one that could erode Liesl's value of honesty (if I covered it up) or build her value of it (if I was willing to get awkward and confess). She easily forgave me, and my hope is that the entire incident had more value than if it had never happened.

Your priorities also have a massive influence. If you decide to make memories together, value time with your family, choose family over your job, spend time and attention in conversation, and charge fearlessly into family tensions with confidence that love and faith will hold you through them, the impact will happen (whether it looks like it or not). If your daughter sees this priority in your life day after day, week after week, she will likely end up wanting it for herself.

When you realize a change needs to be made in your personal life, your family life, or your child's life, you proceed by making one-degree changes. Little by little, inch by inch, you adjust and keep going. Your daughter sees your perseverance and becomes a person who strives for the same kind of growth.

Or maybe you're realizing that you haven't been the best example to your daughter. Our failings as parents have a big influence as well.

My (Brooklyn) parents went through some valleys in their relationship. I'm grateful that they are still together today. But my familiarity with my parents' relationship greatly influenced me to want the opposite. And I've committed to adjust certain things to ensure my marriage is protected.

When you're ready to give up—tired, angry, bitter—your daughter is also watching. Moments like these happen for all of us, but your response to these experiences and feelings makes the most difference. Are you honest about the pain, or do you sweep it under the rug? Do you accept responsibility (and sometimes consequences) for your part in the drama, or do you blame others? Does your daughter get to see you make adjustments and course corrections? Whatever you do and however you respond, it'll be more likely that she'll pattern the same.

You are her starting point. Her point of reference. Even when she is in her car looking back at your house as she heads off to college, she'll be thinking of you. As she sits in a car on her first date, you'll cross her mind. When she's taking a test or talking about her future, things you have said or done will affect her. This is why we need to dream with our girls, talk honestly, and live our lives as an open book in their presence.

If this feels like a big responsibility, that's because it is! But it's a responsibility in the context of God's grace and provision for you as a parent.

Friends and Frenemies

"I always thought it would be boys that would be breaking her heart. I was wrong. Other girls and the drama they sometimes share was much worse."
—Christy; Southlake, Texas

There's been lots of talk about mean girls over the last couple of decades. Books written. Movies produced. But there is nothing like experiencing this in your daughter's life. Whether it's your daughter becoming the mean one or finding herself on the receiving end, it's painful. Either way, observing meanness causes anxiety for parents. And once again, we rely on our support systems to coach us through it, trusting God to give us wisdom in each unique and delicate situation.

Emotionally, she is developing. Changing hormones mixed with continuing cognitive development and shifting social dynamics is a strong cocktail of ups and downs for your daughter's friendships.

Help your daughter handle name-calling. The one dagger that friends and frenemies (a word describing girls who *say* they're friends but treat your daughter as an enemy) both use is name-calling, and it's rampant among teenage girls. Choice words, said out of unbridled emotion, can leave tattooed memories that last a lifetime.

One of my (Brooklyn) very best friends—through childhood and into our teen years—called me a name, and it wounded me deeply. We still hung out, but we mostly ignored each other. Unable to cut off our friendship but unable to move on, we struggled. Her perceptive mom finally called us on it. That's when my emotional volcano erupted and I spewed what had happened. She and I had differing versions of the same story. Our young friendship was tainted, and we never regained the same trust in each other.

All it took was a word.

Help your daughter in her friendships. Help her to be honest and kind. Help her understand the shifting sand of teenage friendships.

You'll likely notice (or have already noticed) a change in your daughter's friendships when she steps into her teen years. That's because children usually form friendships based on proximity (you and I are friends because we live near each other or spend time in the same place). But as your daughter develops new ways of thinking, she starts to differentiate herself from others. And the process that psychologists call *individuation* leads to choosing friends based on affinity (you and I are friends because we like the same things).

When she's choosing friends, help your daughter see that it's valuable to hang out with people different from her. It's great to have a close friend, but it's also good to be inclusive and caring about those who aren't just like you.

Honesty and kindness form the perfect recipe for a growing teen girl. The most socially, emotionally, spiritually stable girls in our youth groups come from homes where honesty and kindness are modeled. It has rubbed off on them, and they find themselves genuinely liking others—even if they aren't anything like they are!

We want our daughters to be able to say, "No, thank you," "I don't really feel comfortable," and "I appreciate the invite, but I won't be able to attend." What empowering statements! What we don't want is for them to say things like, "No, I don't like those people" or fabricate lies about why they don't want to spend time with certain people. Teaching a girl to have grace and tact and to be lovingly honest will be big wins for her in life and in her confidence.

Teenagers across the board will stand in tightly formed circles based on affinities, shared values, and interests. It can be tough getting even the most extroverted teenagers to turn around to see others, noticing those who aren't in the group. Cliques are both a good thing and a bad thing, in our eyes. On one hand, they're an important place of belonging, but they can be horribly destructive (to both those inside and those outside) when the clique is exclusive and dismissive of outsiders. It's important to help a girl see when her friendship group is a good thing and when it's causing drama or pain.

Do They Have a Background Check?

"When your daughter tells you not to get involved with an issue she is having in school because 'she can handle it,' in love, get involved anyway! You may have regrets if you don't. Do some homework on your end. If you think she can handle it, let her. If you think it's too big for her, get involved

even if she doesn't want you to. She will thank you later,
even if she doesn't agree at the moment."
—Kelly; Columbus, Ohio

Your daughter will certainly experience wonderful adults who enter into her world, speaking life and truth over her. They will give great advice. They will mentor her. They will inspire her.

There will be times when she listens to these adults more than she listens to you. There may be times when she compares you to other adults (even if unfairly). Don't waste your energy being threatened by this.

You want these adults to be good influences. You want them to give sound teaching. And you want to make sure they're safe (which includes physical safety, but is more than that).

Some of the adults in your daughter's life are "prescreened" people you know and trust, and there is no question about their level of influence.

However, as your daughter is separating from you and becoming her own person, she will, of course, meet plenty of new adults. This happens through school, extracurricular activities, church, and friendship circles.

Don't be afraid to ask questions and to be in the know:

- Do they have a background check?

- How long have they been teaching?

- What is their experience?

- What is their background?

- Do they seem to have the best interests of your daughter in mind?

It's OK to set boundaries with new adults, new influences in your daughter's life. You are the gatekeeper in many ways.

You won't be able to know everything about everyone. And sometimes, sadly, people you think you can trust aren't actually trustworthy. (Here's that trusting God thing again.) But being proactive and involved will give your daughter the assurance she needs that she's safe.

Does your church do background checks on its leaders? What are the methods and attitudes of coaches and teachers your daughter spends time with?

By the way, it's OK to tag along (even if your daughter says it makes you seem like a "creeper"). Let her know that you'll only stay until you are comfortable with the program or person involved. Your daughter may need that extra support at first until she feels she can trust the leaders and people she's going to be around. As she gets older and nears adulthood, you'll do this less and less, but she still needs your wisdom and experience to give her confidence as she's learning to assess things on her own.

Discussing Dating

Your little girl wants to go to a movie? With a boy? Alone?

You knew the day would come, and now it's here: The little one who only cared about hanging out with her girlfriends is now interested in dating guys.

Once you've picked yourself up off the floor, you've got two choices:

- Find the boy of interest and use scare tactics

- Open up communication with your daughter and keep it open

We all know that scare tactics, while making us feel better, don't really help. And in the long run, you'll damage your relationship with your daughter, forfeiting the opportunity to speak into her life.

So, let's go with the second option when it comes to dating: learning how to communicate.

The scenario above is a common parenting math equation. Teenage girl + teenage guy + movie theater = parent nightmare/potential disaster/cause for high blood pressure.

I (Brooklyn) know this because I was that girl in a movie theater, and I thought it was completely *fine* to be in a movie alone with a boy. So I went, without mentioning to my parents that that my movie included a romantic interest. Double-dating gave me a friend to name-drop so they didn't suspect anything and I could do my own thing. The problem with this was that once on the date, I was never again so confident. What if I couldn't control the situation anymore?

What if I didn't want to do something the guy wanted to do? If only my parents had asked a few clarifying questions (open communication), it would have given me a needed "out" or given them enough information to judge whether or not I should have been on the date in the first place.

And I (Marko) know this because I've been that parent whose daughter was interested in *yet another* boy and wanted to (understandably, really) spend time with him. But how do I (with my wife, and in conversation with my daughter) figure out what boundaries are appropriate? How do I release the fear I'm experiencing and allow for some reasonable freedom? How do I walk alongside my daughter through this experience (and the dozens or hundreds to come) in a way that protects her and still honors her growing need for independence?

The problem, of course, is that teenagers don't usually seek or desire input on their plans. That's because they know you'll find *flaws* in their plans. You will see red flags. You will ask too many questions. But this is the responsibility and role you should have—it's healthy and good, and you can have a great conversation without being the constant downer.

It's important to start and keep open communication flowing. Teenage girls who already have good and open communication with their parents know that their parents love them. They know their parents wouldn't have let them step into situations they expected to be harmful or too risky. However, these girls also want to be trusted.

Clearly, there needs to be some sort of middle ground between "whatever you want" and "no dating until you're 28." There can be good, positive, uplifting exchanges as you ask for insight into your daughter's life, keeping in mind that there will be times when a flag needs to be thrown out there—only because it's what you believe is best for her, not what's necessarily best for you—to keep her safe and make it clear that you care for her and have her best interests in mind.

If you want to help your daughter steer the course through these hormone-rich years, start talking. Try to keep yourself from defaulting into parent lecture mode (which is rarely helpful or productive). She's likely heard about teen pregnancy and about STDs. If she hasn't, please find ways to share with her in an atmosphere that isn't confrontational but is educational, and with care that comes from your heart. And if she doesn't know about God's vision for purity, show her the way through Scripture, or find a good book on the topic to read together.

If a moment presents itself when you get to have a long conversation, then of course, have it! Otherwise, launch conversations with questions like these:

- What sort of person do you want to date? Why?

- What kind of qualities do you hope a date or a potential boyfriend will have?

- What sort of advice would you give a girl who is interested in the guy you like?

- What boundaries do you think will help you stay true to who you are and the kind of relationship you'd like to have?

This final question—the one about boundaries—is super-critical! Make sure you speak into this one yourself, unless your daughter has set boundaries you're completely comfortable with.

We're just going to "hang out"

Define "hang out" by asking great questions. "Hanging out" can mean lots of things, from bowling or walking around a mall, all the way to sitting in a dark room watching a movie with no adult in sight. The term *hanging out* is void of structure—leaving too many variables for a hormone-induced mind to make the best choices, particularly if boundaries aren't already predetermined. And remember, removing opportunities for trouble helps your daughter!

Discuss plans in advance

The probability of a teenager changing her plans midstream at least once a week is roughly between 100 percent and 150 percent. She walks into a movie, watches three minutes, decides it's boring, and spends the rest of her night wandering around the bookstore with a latte. Because of the ever-changing status of a girl's plans, make sure to discuss dates and ideas in advance as much as you can, to get as much information as possible. And it's *very reasonable* to request that your daughter contact you if plans change.

Run scenarios

Ask your daughter what she might do if she were in a particular situation. What would she do, for instance, if she found herself alone with someone, absent of the agreed-upon supervision? Getting her to articulate a plan for various scenarios will cement these ideas in her mind *much more* than if you merely tell her what she should do.

Give her an out by telling her she can blame rules and boundaries on you. Tell her it's OK to say, "Sorry, but I'm not allowed to be here unless there's an adult around."

Suggest ideas if she's unable to give good feedback. Just getting her wheels turning will help her to avoid situations that could cause her to compromise or to be in danger.

And we can't forget this: You love your daughter more than any other human being loves your daughter. She may feel like this isn't the case when she meets a loving (and cute) boy. She may deny your love and insist that it's not there. But she will see it as you stay consistent and caring in your communication.

Choose to trust

This is a tough one, to be sure. But we have to choose to trust our daughters. Even when she violates that trust, we have to choose to trust again (even though there may be consequences and revised boundaries as a result of the broken trust). We trust her to begin making choices on her own. We trust that the same God who is at work in our lives—perfecting us in Christ—is at work in her life. She may not have a strong faith yet. But God, in grace that comes even before she believes in his power and love, will draw her and keep her and give her opportunities to receive it.

"I have always told my daughters that there isn't anything that we can't handle together. No matter what we face, we have each other, and prayer really does change things."
—Kelly; Columbus, Ohio

Shaping Influences

"When my daughter transitioned from little girl to middle schooler, I no longer took closeness with her for granted. I realized that I needed to be intentional about fostering intimacy. I now pick her up from school every day and spend the first 45 minutes having tea with her so we can dish about the day. I try to stay up on the music she loves, and read books she wants me to read so I can connect with her interests. I sit next to her at church or the movies, so I can put my arm around her or rub her back, at times when she welcomes the physical affection."
—Belle; Boston, Massachusetts

When she was little, it was easy to know what interested your daughter. I (Brooklyn) remember when my youngest sister went through a *Little Mermaid* phase. She watched the movie multiple times a day. It was pretty easy to determine her influences: mom, dad, sisters, brother, and mermaids.

But when girls become teenagers, their interests become harder to gauge. Interests become more private and experiences become shared with others outside the family unit. Some are still obvious, particularly if she's into a time-intensive sport or hobby. But new interests—explorations, really—lie beneath the surface.

How do you know what (and who) is influencing her? Since an awareness of her interests is so central to ongoing open communication and engagement, we parents need to have strategies for listening, watching, and drawing out:

- Ask her. (Duh!)

- What's her favorite app, and why?

- If she could spend her whole weekend doing one thing, what would it be?

- Look at her grades. Where does she seem to thrive at school?

- Who does she talk about?

- Who or what does she defend to the point of argument?

- What hours does she keep?

- What are her most valuable possessions, and why?

- Do you know her favorite memory? (It can tell you quite a bit about what she values.)

- Is her free time spent at any one location? Do you see her drawn to certain spaces?

Finding out some of these things will give you clues to the influences that are shaping your daughter outside of your home.

"One thing we've found very meaningful is periodically having movie nights with old home videos when our middle

schooler can laugh over and reflect on early childhood experiences that she might otherwise have forgotten. Those family movie nights are often a springboard for discussions when we reflect on our lives—special vacations, funny or poignant moments."

—Ting (a dad); Boston, Massachusetts

CHAPTER 3: SHE FEELS

Big Blowups

"Raising a teenage daughter is like riding an emotional roller coaster. At first you tend to go up and down with them, and it wears you out. Stay calm and in the middle, and it is better for both of you! Trust me, you can't keep up, and it only makes the situation worse."
—Christy; Southlake, Texas

We've already referenced the sudden shift that most parents experience. But there's almost nowhere that you'll experience this more profoundly than in your daughter's emotional development. It might not appear to happen quite this quickly to an outside observer, but from your vantage point, if *feels* like you're having regular, open dialogue one day, and the next, you find her in her room, on her phone, texting, or online, uninterested in the things you used to share.

Emotional separation from you is a healthy sign that she's becoming more independent. Just because she isn't as excited to spend time with you doesn't mean you don't have a strong relationship with her. Try to respect her in this and take advantage of the opportunities you still have to connect.

Strong relationships between parents and daughters often parallel daughters who are able to have strong peer relationships—they'll be able to discuss their emotions with their peers and learn how to have multiple friends.

Your daughter might be a rare exception, but usually, at some point, the emotional volcano will erupt. Causes might be a clear experience: a friend who isn't able to accept a broadening of the friendship circle, parents who aren't able to accept the movement away from themselves as emotional anchor, or an emotional investment in something or someone not able or willing to return the favor (a relationship, or trying out for a team or role). But sometimes, the root or cause of an emotional blowup is less than clear—even to your daughter!

Add in a dash of "I don't agree with what you've chosen to wear," and a pinch of "You don't know my friends, so how can you tell me they're not OK to hang out with?" Mix in a cup of strong pressure to perform or participate, and an entire batch of technology that speaks, shares, and updates faster than we can think.

You've got a big blowup on your hands.

What do you do when it happens?

How do you talk to your daughter when she starts to shut down or spill over uncontrollably?

We've offered a few suggestions in the following pages. But ultimately, you will need to figure out what works best for your situation. Feel free to adjust as needed.

"I think the biggest thing I've learned through raising teenage girls is to love unconditionally. This sounds simple, but it's really challenging and can't happen without hours of prayer. When your child is in a relationship that you know is dangerous, when you just want to lock her up to keep her safe, when you see the self-loathing and the pain in her eyes and you want to return to those days when she was little and innocent and totally dependent, that's when unconditional love has to kick in. You may want to scream and shake her and tell her she's being stupid, but instead you have to hug her, take walks with her, and try to get her

to open up. Sometimes you may have to sit on the sidelines and watch as she walks through the fire, trusting that her Father will be waiting on the other side. Prayer sustains us as parents, gives us wisdom and hope, placing within our hearts the love that goes beyond human parental love. Prayer makes us more like Christ, enabling us to love even when we are frustrated, angry, and brokenhearted. When our physical eyes see rebellion and hatefulness, prayer enables us to see a confused, hurt little girl. We see her the way God sees her, and we just want to hold her and love her in spite of herself. Love her no matter what she does. She needs to know that there is someone in the world who will never forsake her. That is what will lead her to the heart of the Father."

—Trish (mother of five teenage girls); Lakeland, Florida

Experiment With Times and Spaces

It was Valentine's Day. I (Brooklyn) was driving through Chick-fil-A® at 6:45 a.m. to get breakfast for my lovelies before they woke up. As I was waiting to order, peering from inside my car into the restaurant, I saw something that surprised me.

A teenage girl here, a teenager girl there, sitting at tables, one-on-one with what looked like adult-age people, most likely of the parent type, eating and talking with animation. At 6:45 a.m.?

I realize every teenager is different, and some may not be open to the idea of a pre-day breakfast conversation. But it did strike me as awesome that these parents would care for their girls this way. What I loved so much about this picture was the way the girls' faces lit up as they talked, leaning in, engaging their parents—who sat contentedly listening and enjoying breakfast.

Eating dinner together, asking questions, listening, and leaning in—connecting over a table is a great way to continue in your understanding of your daughter. But maybe not every day is a good day to talk about what just happened over the last 8 to 10 hours.

When I (Brooklyn still) come home from work, the last thing I want to do is rehash my day, at least not right away. I love riding my bike home for this very reason—to get some headspace and distance from whatever I've been focusing in on, be it good or bad or plain ordinary.

We've seen that the same is often true for teenage girls. Give them some room to connect at different times of the day. Maybe your daughter is a morning person who loves breakfast, and it would make her day to spend 15 minutes sharing with you. For certain, a whole lot has gone on in her world in between dinner and breakfast and there will always be something new to share. Other girls are more likely to engage just before bed. Still others open up while riding in the car (but some hate this approach, because they feel trapped).

> *"The first time my daughter tried to fill up the car with gas on her own was a disaster. I received several calls from her in just a few minutes with her crying hysterically. I didn't know what the situation was and feared that she was in real trouble. After several phone calls I learned that she was just frustrated. Being available and calm are necessary through those learning experiences."*
> —Gary; Kansas City, Missouri

Practice One-Word Responses

You may observe that emotions fluctuate when your daughter is dealing with stress. Or you might see a change of behavior a few days before the start of her menstrual cycle. Sometimes she'll be able to handle the stress just fine and you'll be thinking how cool it is to see her grow and mature. But sometimes she'll experience strong emotions that cause her (depending on her personality) to experience wide pendulum swings in a few different emotional directions. If you could remove the emotions from the equation, she could probably figure out the dilemma on her own, but emotions can be blinding and can cause borderline hysterical responses.

What can you do? Try actively listening by acknowledging her feelings with a word or a sound rather than giving advice right away. When it occurs to her at 6 p.m. that her history project is due tomorrow, you might respond with an "Oh." She keeps talking. "I'm not even halfway done!" You could offer up a "Whoa" or a "Hmm" or an "Ah." When she whines that it messes up her plans and she may not be able to go to the movie, your "Ugh" is an empathetic response that helps her feel understood—and could possibly free her to focus on what she needs to do next. "I guess I have to stay home to finish the project; I'll get a lower grade if I'm late."

Answering with an "I see" or an "I get it" empowers your daughter to process some things on her own while having the emotional support she needs from you as a parent.

An unhelpful reaction when she wakes up to the fact that her project is due would be to say, "Don't tell me you've still haven't finished," or "That's what happens when you don't use your planner," or "You'd better get working on it right now." These types of responses start from a critical posture and dismiss worry that is healthy by ignoring—bypassing her own concern—and by telling her what to do. When we do this, we make it harder for our daughter to tell herself what to do. We don't acknowledge her feelings or give her a chance to work out a solution on her own.

This is something we have to work on in youth ministry, too. When a student shows up to our paintball event without a medical release form after we've told them countless times that they need one—well, we can jump to unhelpful responses quickly! It's tempting to say, "I reminded you so many times!" or "You should have listened!" But what they really need to hear from us are things like "Oh," "Ugh," and "What do you think we should do?"

Helping your daughter sort out her emotions and make decisions in the midst of them could be one of the greatest gifts you can give to her. It'll help her with friends, in her jobs, in her education. And most of all, it will help her to feel valued by you.

"I have often reflected back on the first few minutes of my daughter's life when I held her in my arms and bathed her in the delivery room. Remembering those moments of being

overwhelmed with love and responsibility was a source of strength and encouragement through the challenging times."

—Gary; Kansas City, Missouri

When Emotions Flow Both Ways

It's not a secret that teenagers can make parents angry— or that parents can make teenagers angry! There's a natural tension between very different family members, particularly when one of them is learning to differentiate and become more autonomous. Parents and teenagers aren't always moving at the same pace, so it's good to have a few approaches in mind when the tension builds and you find yourself in a negative, annoying, irritating, or even infuriating place of tension.

Be slow to speak and quick to listen. This biblical truth will help you make better communication choices when you're in the middle of an emotional situation. Reflecting before reacting gives you time to think about what you're about to say and why. It doesn't have to be a long period of time, just long enough to discern the best direction and to quiet your own emotions.

We've learned, working with teenagers, that it's better to focus on how we're feeling in a frustrating situation rather than focusing on how wrong they are (they usually figure that out on their own, later). When we share how we're feeling, they are more likely to hear what we're saying. Telling a teenager in one of our ministries that her lying made us feel like she doesn't trust us has opened the door for her to listen without feeling attacked.

Her lie, while still wrong, can become a learning experience, a moment when she realizes what she's done and attempts to make it right.

You'll never get every conversation right with your daughter—there will be moments when you feel embarrassed and ashamed for reacting or responding poorly. However, those serve as great opportunities for you to show her how you're growing, too!

At the End of the Day

No matter what emotions she's experiencing, remind your daughter often that God is the creator of our emotions. They're given to us to help us grasp how wide and how deep and how long is the love of Christ. They're given to us to perceive needs. They're given to us to be an indicator of what's going on in our minds and in our hearts. They're given to us so that, in God's great love for us, we can experience the fullness of life Jesus promises (John 10:10).

Encourage your daughter—give her moments to let her emotions soar or roar. This may mean letting her cry her eyes out as she enters your car at the end of a bad day. It may mean laughing hysterically together with her. It might even mean being angry with her for a time. Give her guidance and help her see who she really is: a wonderfully special person.

CHAPTER 4: SHE CELEBRATES

Making Lasting Memories

"If your daughter, after getting her temporary license on her 16th birthday, runs your car over a curb and into a small tree, go home and tell your husband what happened! Don't cover it up (by taking the blame). This is how she'll grow and learn."
—*Kelly (Brooklyn's mom); Columbus, Ohio*

I (Brooklyn) am about to do something that violates Girl Code. I'm going to divulge top-secret information for the sake of helping parents understand their daughters.

Over the last decade, a circle of a few hundred girls has held sacred the information I'm about to share. They may never forgive me for revealing tradition—and if one of you is reading this, remember, there are some things that will *never* be revealed and you will carry on the tradition someday with your own girls, for sure!

In my earlier days of youth ministry, I would say I was unashamedly adventurous in my approach to celebrating our girls, their changes, and the things that make them different from the guys.

At summer camp one night, I decided to call all of the girls in the dorm into the common area for a very "serious" talk. I came prepared with a giant box of tampons (cue the awkwardness), a stereo, and some very inspirational music.

What they thought: "We're in trouble."

What I thought: "I could be in trouble, but I'm doing it anyway."

My goals: (1) Turn awkward into awesome, (2) unite the sixth- through 12th-graders in Girl Code, and (3) embarrass myself so badly that every girl going to sleep that night would feel awesome about herself.

I had prepped a couple of my more mature seniors to follow my lead—to do what I did—and to just trust me.

Starting with a serious face, I told everyone to stand up and to forget about free time tomorrow…(long pause)…because we were going to have free time tonight!

Cue Whitney Houston's slow building song "Step by Step" where I led the girls in finger aerobics (don't ask) and then into freak-out dancing (another don't ask) and then into singing with tampon or hairbrush microphones (ridiculously silly, and for some of the younger girls, flat-out shocking). Then we—well, I can't tell you the fun we had next because it's the most secret of all secrets and I would never be forgiven if I went any further in this. Let's just say: Our girl freak-out party happened every year after that, always at an unexpected and unannounced time.

This crazy little celebration, for many of our girls, was the rite of passage that defined their summer camp experience, connected them with other girls, and made them feel at home in their changing bodies and unpredictable emotions and friendships. It also created a memory linked to their faith journey. I never really thought all of that out in the beginning, but the outcomes over the years yielded these things. And I'm a believer that shared moments like this do give extra glue to the message you offer with your life and your love.

Here's a short, abridged list of some of the reasons our family (Marko here) has found to create a celebration with Liesl, who's now 18 years old: starting middle school, her first period, getting a lead role in a play, starting high school, acceptance into a city-wide youth orchestra, a good grade in a hard class, successful completion of a huge school project, getting her driver's permit, getting her driver's license, her first college acceptance letter. And dozens more. Celebrations might look like Liesl getting to choose her favorite carryout for our family dinner (Thai food), or something more extravagant. But we love to celebrate.

Celebrating milestones and making memories with your daughter is a great way to understand her, open dialogue, and create positive memories.

Parents are usually pretty good about remembering and celebrating birthdays. Start with that (even if you haven't succeeded in recent years). She might hope to have a birthday celebration with her friends, one you're *not* a part of, so have two celebrations—one for your family, one for her friends. It's not about how much money you spend. It's about finding ways to see her and share your love for the person she is and is becoming.

Celebrate Faith Milestones

Make the moments of her baptism, confirmation, or faith decisions a big deal. A "big deal" could be dinner together at her favorite restaurant, a weekend away, or a photo and a handwritten letter. Just something to commemorate her journey in faith.

Maybe you've heard the strange Bible word *Ebenezer* (or you might know it from the hymn that says, "Here I raise my Ebenezer"). An Ebenezer was a pile of rocks, a little impromptu monument to mark, "This is a place where God met us." We like to think that the celebrations your family creates about spiritual moments in your daughter's life will become Ebenezers, spiritual mile markers on her faith journey. Looking back, she will remember the celebrations, and they will (or at least *can*) remind her of the spiritually significant moments and choices behind them.

Break Out a Smile

When she surprises you in a good way, show your surprise and give her the response that you are truly feeling. Allow her to experience your joy, to see your pride, and to feel your love and respect.

Reward her heart. When you see her giving of herself in unselfish ways, serve her and thank her and acknowledge that you see a kingdom-hearted individual growing up.

When she makes a good choice or displays a great attitude, mention it—don't just recognize it and hold it in your heart!

The other day, my daughter (Marko) said to my wife and me, "Thanks for being such cool parents." While I don't care so much about being perceived as cool, I know what she meant. She meant that she sees our effort, that she knows we love her and believe in her, that we *trust* her. Those, of course, are words we would not have heard from her when she was 15, but they will sustain me through many bumps and fears throughout her young adult years.

When your daughter looks back, as she walks away from your home with courage as her new, independent self, let your voice be the first voice she hears cheering her along toward healthy friendships, solid faith, and embracing who God made her to be.

Your daughter is a gift, a glorious one-of-a-kind miracle. She carries your DNA and has been shaped by you in countless ways. She carries a piece of your faith and the example you've set before her. But she is individually loved by her Creator, who has a unique vision for her life (and always has, from before the beginning of time).

Enjoy this time you have to care for her and invest in her.

Check out all the books in our
PARENT'S GUIDE Series!

A Parent's Guide to Understanding **Teenage Guys**
A Parent's Guide to Understanding **Teenage Girls**
A Parent's Guide to Understanding **Sex & Dating**
A Parent's Guide to Understanding **Teenage Brains**
A Parent's Guide to Understanding **Social Media**

Visit SimplyYouthMinistry.com to learn more
about each of these books!